Jibber Jabber Jumpers Stan's Baby Pepper Steppers MiNi SOUL STARS

HOT SHOTS EBONY ANGELS Skipperoos Jibber Jabber Jumpers Stan's MiN

ERWIND SKIPPERS Bouncing Bulldogs HOT SHOTS EBONY ANGELS Jabber J

UL STARS Lucky Leapers Mo Money Honeys SUMMERWIND SKIPPERS MiNi SOUL STARS Lucky

GELS Skipperoos Jibber Jabber Jumpers Stan's Baby Pepper Steppers MiNi SOUL STARS Lucky Le

Jibber Jabber Jumpers Stan's Baby Pepper Steppers MiNi SOUL STARS Lucky Leapers Mo Money H

HOT SHOTS EBONY ANGELS Skipperoos Jibber Jabber Jumpers Stan's Baby Pepper Steppers MiN

ERWIND SKIPPERS Bouncing Bulldogs HOT SHOTS EBONY ANGELS Skipperoos Jibber Jabber

UL STARS Lucky Leapers Mo Money Honeys SUMMERWIND SKIPPERS MiNi SOUL STARS Lucky L

GELS Skipperoos Jibber Jabber Jumpers Stan's Baby Pepper Steppers MiNi SOUL STARS Lucky Le

Jibber Jabber Jumpers Stan's Baby Pepper Steppers MiNi SOUL STARS Lucky Leapers Mo Money H

HOT SHOTS EBONY ANGELS Skipperoos Jibber Jabber Jumpers Stan's Baby Pepper Steppers MiN

ERWIND SKIPPERS Bouncing Bulldogs HOT SHOTS EBONY ANGELS Skipperoos Jibber Jabber J

UL STARS Lucky Leapers Mo Money Honeys SUMMERWIND SKIPPERS MiNi SOUL STARS Lucky L

GELS Skipperoos Jibber Jabber Jumpers Stan's Baby Pepper Steppers MiNi SOUL STARS Lucky L

Jibber Jabber Jumpers Stan's Baby Pepper Steppers MiNi SOUL STARS Lucky Leapers Mo Money H

HOT SHOTS EBONY ANGELS Skipperoos Jibber Jabber Jumpers Stan's Baby Pepper Steppers MiN

ERWIND SKIPPERS Bouncing Bulldogs HOT SHOTS EBONY ANGELS Skipperoos Jibber Jabber J

UL STARS Lucky Leapers Mo Money Honeys SUMMERWIND SKIPPERS MiNi SOUL STARS Lucky L

DOUBLE DUTCH

A Celebration of Jump Rope, Rhyme, and Sisterhood

VERONICA CHAMBERS

JUMP AT THE SUN

HYPERION BOOKS
FOR CHILDREN

NEW YORK

For Arthur and Louise,
with love

ACKNOWLEDGMENTS

This book was blessed with many angels. I'd like to thank Jason Clampet for help with research, editing, cooking, driving, and, when necessary, turning. He's double-handed, but flawless in every other way.

My agent, Sandy Dijkstra, and her coworkers, Margaret Porter Troupe, Elisabeth James, and Julie Burton, are all double-Dutch divas. Andrea Davis Pinkney had the vision and got the game started.

Debbie Egan-Chin, Oscar Perez, Ron Tarver, Malaika Adero, and Deborah Willis provided wonderful photographs. A special shout-out to Deb Willis, who in work and life continues to teach and inspire me. Thank you.

Many thanks to Debra Jackson for her research, insight, and ideas.

Chikage provided much needed translation with the double-Dutch interviews. Ruri Kawashima and the Japan Society are, as always, a treasure trove of resources. *Domo arrigato gozaimasu!*

Many fine writers and creative types gave input into the "Double Dutch Is . . ." section. These include: Elizabeth Alexander, Lynette Clemetson, Peggy Orenstein, Melissa Giraud, Farai Chideya, Shay Youngblood, Martha Redbone, John Singleton, Ruth Forman, and Tahira Reid.

Thank you to the double-Dutch friends featured here: Jenny and Lily, Rodney and Desiree, Erika and Adrienne.

Finally, I'd like to thank the girls of Beverly Road—my childhood double-Dutch girls. They taught me how to jump for joy.

INTRODUCTION 6

SEEING DOUBLE 8

JUMPING IN! 19
A Double-Dutch History

24

DOUBLE DUTCH IS . . .

TAHIRA REID 38
Double Dutch's Answer to Ben Franklin

TURNING JAPANESE! 43

DOUBLE-DUTCH FRIENDSHIP 51

DOUBLE LONGING 57
An Excerpt from *Mama's Girl*

INTRODUCTION
BY TONYA LEWIS LEE

ANYONE WHO has witnessed double Dutch knows that to be a part of the double-Dutch game means that you belong to a special group. Warmth and sisterhood instantly come to mind. Young girls are connected for at least a moment to the rhythm of their steps and to each other. For that moment everything is in sync and all is right with the world. When I see the images of young girls jumping, I remember the heat of the summers of my youth, the attitude of the girls who jumped, their strength and ability. I am reminded of a happy time and feel gratified to see that this expression of girlhood continues to evolve. Thankfully, this significance has been recognized and documented. For there is no better symbol of girl power than double Dutch.

Throughout this collection of wonderful photos, the look on the face of each girl reflects the same sentiment: they are serious, focused, and in a zone, working together. The strength of each young woman is not just in her obvious athletic ability as she does handstands or spins while still jumping, but also in the support she gives the others. No one can get good at double Dutch working alone. You learn from your sisters, you grow with the help of your sisters, and you teach and encourage your friends. This is a lesson that clearly must remain with each girl in her life beyond the days of double Dutch.

Throughout this book we repeatedly hear stories of how double Dutch was the spark that ignited a new relationship or the glue that kept a friendship going. We are reminded of this unspoken language that breaks the awkward silence of a new friendship. When a girl brings out her ropes or begins a classic chant there is that instant bond over a rhythm that seems ancient. Double Dutch is the club you join because of your strength, skill, and ability to be part of a team, nothing else required.

As my daughter and I read through this book together, she became more and more anxious to master double Dutch, to have fun, to focus on and be a part of this very special group of strong young women. The energy of the photographs and the emotion of the essays affirm that girl power is strong and alive, and that double Dutch rules!

d o u • b l e _a d j ._

1 : having a twofold relation or character: dual

2 : consisting of two, usually combined, members

or parts ⟨an egg with a double yolk⟩

3 : being twice as great or many

4 : of extra size, strength, or value— ⟨a double

martini⟩

5 : of rhyme, involving correspondence of

two syllables ⟨as in _exciting_ and

inviting—just like this book!⟩

6 : designed for two persons ⟨a double

room; a double bed⟩

Designed for two people, that's how I think of
this book. It's a book to be shared between
friends, mothers and daughters, blood
sisters, play sisters, and soul sisters.

ALL in together, **GIRLS!**
How do you like the
weather, **GIRLS?**
When it's your **BIRTHDAY,**
please **JUMP** in. . . .
January, February,
MARCH, April,
MAY . . .

I've jumped double Dutch all my life. I feel as if I came out of the womb with my sneakers laced up and ready to jump rope! But my mother says this couldn't possibly be so. I was five years old when we moved to Brooklyn, New York—the unofficial double-Dutch capital of the Western world. So I think it's safe to assume I started jumping then, which was exactly twenty-five years ago.

Wow.

ALL **OUT** together, **GIRLS**!
HOW do you **like** the
weather, **GIRLS**?
When it's your **BIR+HDAY**,
please **JUMP** **OUT**....
January, February,
MARCH, April,
MAY . . .

It usually takes two people to turn the rope, but when it was getting late and nobody else was around, my friend Jeanine and I would just tie a rope to our fence so we could still jump.

The rope would be wobbly, but we didn't care. We were double-Dutching fools. When there was too much snow outside on the ground, we jumped inside the toolshed. Once, we even moved all the tables and chairs and tried to jump in the dining room. But the rope kept hitting the chandelier and I was too afraid of breaking it, so we stopped! We'd jump anyplace, night or day. We were jumping double Dutch and we weren't by ourselves, we were together. We were a double. Extra size. Extra strength. Extra value.

Good things come in doubles—not just the double ropes you need to turn double Dutch, but double scoops of ice cream, double dates, double-decker buses, and double-decker sandwiches. Even double agents in spy movies can be really cool, especially when they're wearing double-breasted suits! Double stars are two stars that are so close together, they look like they're stuck—like Siamese twins—but they're not. They're separate, but very close. Just like Jeanine and me.

Jumping double Dutch was, and is, to me the epitome of girlhood. (Though some boys jump double Dutch, too!) But when I think about that time when I jumped double Dutch, I think about myself and my home girls.

Jeanine lived downstairs from me in a red-brick, three-family house that had a big yard, a hydrangea tree, and a tall fence. She was tall, with skin the color of a tree branch. Because we lived in the same house, we were best friends. But we were always fighting and making up. Sometimes, it seemed that Jeanine was always in charge: she'd decide what games we'd play, what we'd eat for lunch, who we'd hang out with. But then, sometimes, I'd muster up a little courage and form an "I hate Jeanine" club and invite everyone to join. Except, of course, Jeanine. This would last until Jeanine and I made up, and I'd vote to disband the club. Someone would second the motion. And everybody would say, "Aye," rolling their eyes at the thought that I'd even made them participate in such a stupid, petty thing.

Jackie, who was from London, moved to the neighborhood when I was about ten years old. She was a serious challenge to my double-Dutch throne. Not only was she older and beautiful and spoke with an accent that everyone thought was sooo cool, but Jackie could jump. Who knew British girls could jump double Dutch like that? Not me.

Sharon and her little sister, Jeanette, lived around the corner. It was always

Fire. Fire.
FALSE ALARM.
(GiRL'S NAME) fell into
(Boy's name) arms
Is he the **one** whose
kisses are HOT?
Maybe he is.
Maybe he's not.
Yes, no, **maybe so.**
Yes, no, maybe so.

great when they came to play, because that meant the minute they knocked on my door we had enough girls to play—two to turn, one to jump.

Drena lived across the street from me. Her uncle worked for the telephone company, and, as everybody knows, telephone wire is the best kind of double-Dutch rope. It's light but strong, and when it hits the ground, it sings—*rat, tat, tat, tat*—like rain on a windowpane or Max Roach tearing up the drums on an old-school jazz record. Drena had the best rope, which meant Drena had power.

Tracie lived in the old Victorian next door. It was massive and white with peeling black trim. Back then, I thought her house was impossibly elegant and stately, like something out of a movie.

All the girls said Tracie's house was haunted. Maybe it was because inside, everything was covered with dust, and the backyard looked like something out of a junkyard or *Sanford and Son*. There were broken toys and heaps of metal from stoves and refrigerators and cars. The boys in the neighborhood said there were bodies buried beneath those cars, but they could never prove it.

Tracie lived in that house with a gang of brothers and sisters, so many that

George Washington never told a LiE. Till he ran **around** the **corner and** *Stole* a cherry pie. How many **cherries** were in **THAT** pie? 1, 2, 3, 4, 5, 6, 7, 8, 9 . . .

we could hardly keep track. We knew she had a mother and a father, but we never saw them.

Tracie had dark doe's eyes that looked like she'd woken up with a fresh application of black eyeliner, even though she hadn't. She was pretty in a sad kind of way, like a black-and-white picture of a girl who's lost her sweetheart in a war. She never complained about turning, like the rest of us. When you handed her the rope, she just said thank you.

I think that Tracie loved jumping rope so much because she had no toys besides the junk in the yard: no games, no cards, no nothing. Even the day after Christmas, when all the girls had gathered at Drena's

DOWN in the valley,
where the green
grass grows,
There sat (Girl's name)
pretty as a rose.
Up came (Boy's name) and
KISSED her on the cheek.
How many kisses did
she get this week?

to show off their loot, Tracie came empty-handed. She didn't even bring a sweater or a scarf, given by a mean old aunt who was too stupid to know that what a girl wanted was toys, not clothes. Instead, on that day, Tracie played with one of Drena's old dolls while we played with our new Barbies and their accessories. After a couple of hours, Penthouse Barbie drove off in her new red Corvette for her first date with Malibu Ken after getting into a huge fight with Skipper over who owned the purple sweater and matching leg warmers that Barbie wanted to wear on her date.

"What do we do now?" Drena moaned. As the richest girl in our group, Drena was always the one who got bored the quickest.

It was Tracie who stood up and said, "Let's play double Dutch." And that's what we did.

There were other girls who sometimes joined our games. Iris was a Puerto Rican girl who lived across the street. She was probably no more than seventeen, but she seemed to be thirty. She had full, round breasts and hips to spare. She flirted with boys and called them *"Papi"*—a name that never failed to lift their shoulders and crinkle their lips into a proud smile.

Iris smoked cigarettes and didn't bother to put them out when her mother came home from work.

If she was on her stoop, having a puff, and you called out to her and begged, Iris might jump for a few minutes. She might even turn. She was a good jumper and certainly the most worldly girl on the block.

Camille lived across the street, and she was, like her name, elegant and old-worldly. Her mother didn't let her come out to play much. Whenever she did, though, Camille always sat on her porch with a pleasant, slightly bored expression, like a woman in a painting. One thing I knew about her was that her window faced the street where we jumped. I knew this because once after my mother and Camille's mother talked at a party, I was invited to her house to play. Everything in her room was white and looked like something out of a magazine: white canopy bed, white shag rug, white beanbag chair, white lace curtains.

Some summer afternoons, when it was hot and the boys down the street had opened up the fire hydrant and the teenage boys went to play basketball and the teenage girls went to watch them, my friends and I would gather to play a little rope. I'd be standing on the corner, trying to stay cool in tube tops and shorts. There'd be a whole gang of girls waiting to jump, 'cause everybody knew that our

16

DoWN in the **meadow** where the **corn cobs** grow, a grasshopper JUMPED on an **elephant's toe.** The **elephant cried** with tears in his **eyes,** "Why don't you pick on someone **your size?"**

corner was hot on the double-Dutch tip. There'd be two girls turning and maybe five or six girls waiting to jump.

Of course, the girl in the rope would be taking her time. Maybe it was Sharon, or maybe it was Jackie, calling out, "Your mama ain't got no drawers. I'm the one who saw them all," in her singsong Brixton accent. The rest of us would be sweating in the heat, keeping track of the jumper's time: "One up, two, three, four, five, six, seven, eight, nine. Two up, three, four, five, six, seven, eight, nine." We might get to thirty or forty up before Sharon or Jackie would show any signs of slowing down.

I'd be calling out numbers, my eyes wandering to the tops of the trees. And I'd catch a glimpse of Camille's bedroom window. Maybe it was my imagination, or maybe it was the heat making everything look shaky, but it seemed that the white lace curtains would rustle. The curtains would open and close, just like that. I always thought it was Camille up there watching us. Wishing she were outside.

JUMPiNG.

JUMPING IN!
A DOUBLE-DUTCH HISTORY

HUNDREDS OF YEARS AGO, some genius—man, woman, or child, we don't know—took a soft, supple branch of a tree and began to skip, and the tradition of jumping rope was born. People of every color, in almost every nation, have a tradition of jumping rope. According to the American Double Dutch League's rule book, the history of jumping between two twirling ropes dates back to ancient civilizations in Phoenicia, Egypt, and China. Which means Cleopatra might have jumped double Dutch. King Tut and Confucius, too!

MALAIKA ADERO

Double Dutch is said to have been introduced in America by Dutch colonialists, back in the 1600s, when New York was still called New Amsterdam. "Double Dutch" was a negative expression, coined by the English, to describe anything they didn't understand about the Dutch. The game earned its name because the process of creating a helix with ropes, then jumping in between them, was as impossible for the early British settlers as trying to understand someone who spoke "double Dutch."

In nineteenth-century America, only boys jumped rope—girls were too busy playing Miss Mary Mack and other hand-clapping games. Around 1890, girls' fashion got a lot less prissy, opening the way for respectable young ladies to jump high while still keeping their modesty. Girls mixed things up in more ways than one— matching hand-clapping rhymes to the foot-fancy rhythms of jumping rope.

After World War II, double Dutch took to the streets and became as synonymous with city living as games like handball and skully. Yet by the late 1950s, the sport had begun to wane in popularity. It took a Harlem cop named David Walker, who was working as a Community Affairs detective, to set the ropes spinning again

I like **coffee**.
I *like* **tea**.
I like (**Boy's name**)
and he **likes** me.
YES, no, **maybe** so.
Yes, no, maybe **so**.

in New York City. In 1973, Walker was looking for a sport to build confidence and athleticism in the young girls of his Harlem neighborhood. "I saw a group of kids playing in Harlem one day," Walker once told the *Daily News*. "I thought I could add some rules and regulations and make it into a team sport." The tournament that Walker began in 1974 has turned into a world-class event that is held every year at the Apollo Theater in Harlem. The popularity

of double Dutch is so far flung that for three years in a row, the winning team came all the way from Japan. Still, Walker continues to dream of bigger and better things for the sport of double Dutch. He'd like to see it become an event in the Olympics. "That's my ultimate objective before I hang up the ropes."

ROCKETT GIRLS

IT'S EARLY SATURDAY MORNING, and five girls gather in the gymnasium of Reed Junior High School in Central Islip, Long Island. They are a multiracial group: white, black, and brown, but each girl is dressed in a matching red tracksuit. When they jump into the double-Dutch ropes, each head bobs with an identical ponytail. They are a team. And what's more, each girl, averaging only thirteen years old, knows what it's like to be a winner. The Snazzy Steppers, as this team is called, are the New York City champions. They are also ranked fifth in the world.

As they unfold their ropes and begin to jump, they are intensely silent. They don't sing songs; they don't recite rhymes. Peggy and Debbie jump in to rehearse their doubles routine. They move in unison, which isn't easy, and they execute even the most complex moves with a uniform grace. It's as if they were rowers on the same boat, their arms and legs slicing and curving

Call the **Army!**
Call the NAVY!
(Girl's name) got a
CRUSH,
and he's driving her
CRAZY.
He kissed her once.
He kissed her twice.
He gave her some hickies
she couldn't HIDE.
How many hickies
did she GET?

together. The two turners offer up tips and criticism. "Don't go faster than rope," Lanieequah reminds her teammates. Sometimes, the entire team catches a case of the giggles, prompting their coach to insist they focus harder. "I'm not laughing," Peggy mutters. "Yes, you were," whispers Debbie. "I smile and then you laugh."

In the ropes, it seems that the Steppers defy gravity. They do handstands and back-flips. They bend to touch their feet and kick their legs as high as Radio City Rockettes. But they are something even better. They are astronauts of the asphalt, rocket girls limited only by their imagination and their unbelievably limber, athletic bodies.

Life for the Snazzy Steppers wasn't always so sweet. It was only five years ago that these girls couldn't jump double Dutch at all. Their coach, David Rockett, started the team eight years ago when he became frustrated with the lack of positive activities for kids in the

public school where he teaches. "One recess, I was looking out the window of my classroom," says Coach Rockett. "Some of the kids were doing double Dutch on the playground. I was fascinated by the call-and-response element, the rhythms, and the movement." The very next day, Rockett went to the local Home Depot and bought a couple hundred yards of clothesline. He made a flyer inviting students to form a double-Dutch team. Forty girls showed up!

Coach Rockett was thrilled but intimidated. Most of the girls had no double-Dutch experience. He'd have to teach them; but first, he had to learn himself! No small feat for a forty-something white guy from the 'burbs. But Coach Rockett was determined to see his girls fly. He visited other schools and playgrounds, asking kids for lessons. He studied books about jump rope and scanned the Internet for competition tips and news. In just a few short months, he had mastered the game. As he likes to remind his team, "White men can jump!" Coach Rockett even wrote a song to help teach his girls how to jump:

My name is Franny.
I'm the rainbow frog.
Inside the ropes
I'm a double-Dutch star!

Bring three friends together,
who share the same dream.
Two turners and one jumper
make a winning jump-rope team!

Let's start with two ropes,
turners hold the ends.
Don't drop the ropes,
or you'll have to start again.

Bend your knees slightly,
with your feet set apart.
Spin those ropes round and round,
you're off to a good start.

Can you imagine an eggbeater
as it spins round and round?
That's how the ropes look
as they slap on the ground.

Come gather around, friends.
We're going to have some fun
singing and jumping
double Dutch.

Coach Rockett taught the girls
all he knew, and then they attended their first competition in Harlem. The
girls were pulverized. Back in Central Islip, it had seemed that they were so
talented! Everyone at Reed Junior High School was impressed by the way they
could do flips and somersaults in the rope. Sure, at home, the Snazzy Steppers
were so baaaaad, they were good, but the teams in Harlem were faster, bolder,
smoother, and sassier. The girls left Harlem with no trophies and their confidence ripped to pieces. "It was the most painful thing to watch. They thought
they were all that," remembers Coach Rockett. "Then they saw double Dutch
for the first time. The girls hid in the bathroom at the competition, feigning

illness. They were so scared. They knew they were one of the weakest teams in the league."

The Snazzy Steppers were down but by no means out. Each year, they returned to competition a little stronger. First, they won fifth place, then fourth, then third, then second. Finally, after a lot of hard work, they grabbed the number-one spot in New York City, qualifying for the world championships. They've been flying high ever since. They've also become the best of friends. "It's a funny math," says Coach Rockett. "In double Dutch, one plus one plus one doesn't equal three. One plus one plus one equals one. You have to be tight. If you and I are turning and we have even the tiniest bit of animosity toward each other, it comes out on the ropes. You're trying to get kids to care about each other, to learn about each other, to nurture each other. When it works—when a team comes together—it makes for a powerful group of young women."

JACK be nimble.
Jack be quick.
Jack **jumped** over
the **candlestick**.
TWENTY-four,
sixty-nine—
let me see **you**
JUMP
double-time!
Let me see you do the
mumbo, MUMBo,
mumbo.
Let me see you do a
kick, **KICK**, kick.
Let me see you SCISSORS,
scissors, **scissors**.
LET me see **you** do some
splits, splits, **splits**.
Pop-ups, ten to one.
Hit it, and you'll be done:
10, 9, 8, 7, 6, 5, 4, 3, 2, 1!

Each of the Snazzy Steppers has her favorite element of competition:

"Speed is my favorite thing. The challenge of it," says Debbie.

"Freestyle. It's where you get to express yourself," says Erika.

"My favorite thing is . . . the trophies!" says Katelyn.

"My best moment was when I learned the karate kick, when I was in the third grade. It's such an easy trick, but it was my first trick. The first time I ever showed some style in the rope," says Peggy.

"I'm the only girl on the team who came in knowing street double Dutch. It's different from competitive jumping. In street rope, you jump long and fast. In competition, you're slowing down the rope so you can catch the trick. It was almost harder than learning from scratch. My style had to change," says Lanieequah.

DOUBLE DUTCH IS . . .

"... **fearlessness.** The audacious willingness to jump in and mix things up when life is sweeping over you from all sides in incessant, overwhelming waves. The skill—ultimately, the thrill—is not in stopping the flow, but in keeping pace with rhythm."

—Lynette Clemetson, reporter for *The New York Times*

"... **confidence in motion.** Double Dutch is bodies in motion, not decoration: strong, glorious, exultant.

Double Dutch is glorious."

—Peggy Orenstein, award-winning author of *School Girls*

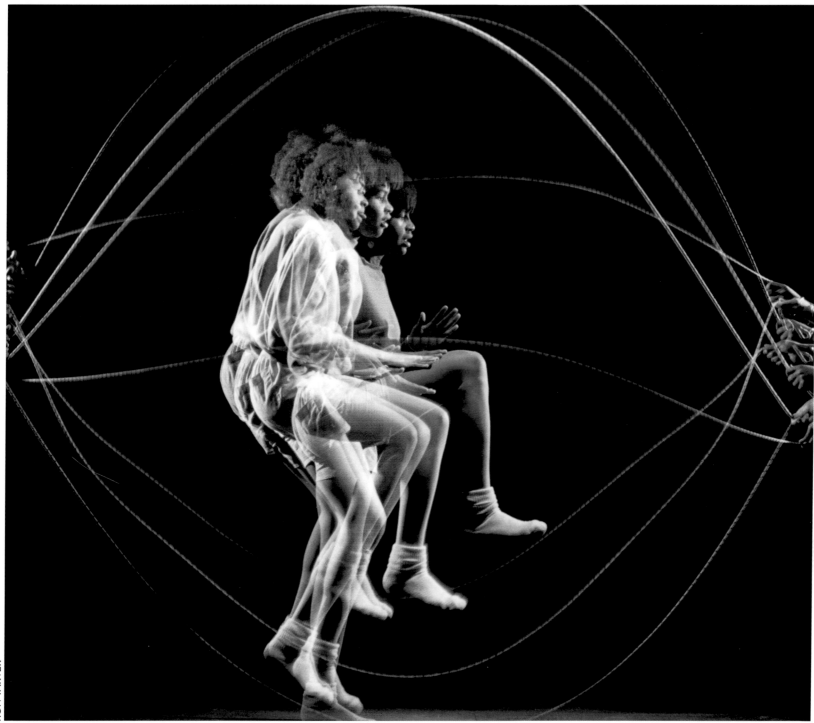

"...for the daring, the fearless girls who moved so fast it looked as if they were in two places at once."

—Shay Youngblood, novelist

"...TRIPPING TWICE. Too quick for me. Concrete against green plastic. *Twack, twack! Twack, twack!* Jumping while crouching because I'm too tall."

—Melissa Giraud, radio producer

"...rhythm, poetry and geometry. Flow."

—Farai Chideya, television correspondent and author

"... life. It is yin and yang. All little black girls continue to play double Dutch throughout adulthood. It's a symbol of how you navigate the good and the bad, the positive and the negative, the ups and downs. Those little baby steps into two ropes are a black girl's pattern of courage for life. Just don't trip."

—John Singleton, filmmaker

"...the connecting of minds, spirits of adventure, togetherness. In the summer of '85, double Dutch was what bonded me to the new neighborhood we moved into. It was the first summer, and the first time I learned to jump with the girls who were so patient and eager to teach. After a while, we didn't need to talk to each other, just jump and rhyme."

—Martha Redbone,
singer-songwriter

" ... **pride**. It means you know how to do something that not everybody knows how to do. People stare in awe when they see you jump double Dutch.

—Tahira Reid, inventor of the automatic double-Dutch machine

" ... **the sidewalk's favorite dance**, 'cuz it gets to sing with us. The ancestors drumming beneath our feet. A way for our sneakers to weave air and fly above rainbows."

—Ruth Forman, poet

" ... *Could not jump like that,* could not rock like that, could not make my legs vanish into a whirr of hummingbird wings with a backbeat, could not be quintessential in the way that double Dutch is (say it!) quintessentially black girl, but nonetheless could love it, feel its wind freshen my face, its beat rock my boat, double Dutch strangely like Gwendolyn Brooks's poems to me now: as precise, as rhythmic, as female, as black, as dazzling, as speed-of-light."

—Elizabeth Alexander, poet

TAHIRA REID

TAHIRA REID WAS an eight-year-old girl living in the Bronx, a borough of New York City, when she came up with her first invention. There was a poster contest for kids in the third grade, and the theme was: "What would you like to see in the future?" It was the year the Space Shuttle *Challenger* was launched, and almost everyone drew a picture of astronauts, rockets, or people who lived on the moon. But Tahira thought an invention should be practical, as well as imaginative. Although she was just a little girl, she had already grasped the credo of history's finest inventors.

As a third grader, Tahira's biggest problem was that she didn't have anyone to turn double Dutch for her when she came home from school. Before, in between, and after classes, she could jump whenever she wanted, surrounded by girls who also loved to turn and jump. In her neighborhood, however, there weren't any kids her age, and Tahira couldn't jump double Dutch alone. She came up with the idea for a machine that would turn the ropes for you. You just push a button, and *voilà*! Two ropes would spin like eggbeaters before you. Tahira's poster won first place in

the contest. She was too little to figure out how to make the machine, though, and just had to jump when she was at school.

Ten years later, Tahira was a student at Rensselaer Polytechnic Institute in Troy, New York, studying mechanical engineering. In one of her first design courses, she was again presented with an inventing problem. Her professor asked her to draw up plans for a machine that challenged the limits of sports. At first, Tahira was stumped. She kept thinking about traditional games such as football and basketball, and she came up with nothing at all. Then she remembered her third-grade poster project. What she knew about football she could squeeze on the head of a pin, but what she knew about double Dutch could fill an entire book.

With a team of fellow students, Tahira invented the automatic double-Dutch machine—a real-life embodiment of her third-grade dream. With this device, ropes

are connected to two wheels on opposing metal posts. After an engine is turned on, the ropes spin into action. Although it took more than a year to get the machine to actually work, Tahira got an A in the course. Even better, her device has been exhibited at museums such as the Smithsonian Institution and featured in newspapers and on television shows across the country. She even holds a patent for her invention. If you go to the U.S. Patent Office in Washington, D.C., you can find her name in the same registry as Ben Franklin: Tahira Reid, inventor of the automatic double-Dutch device. To this day, the thought makes her dreamy. "Everyone paid attention," she says. "I remember thinking, This is a historic moment—no one's ever jumped double Dutch without turners before."

Even now that she's grown up, Tahira still loves to stop and watch when girls in her old neighborhood are playing double Dutch. "It's like a sorority," she says. "You are sisters in this love of double Dutch. When you get together, there are no pretenses or barriers. You all share these happy memories of being girls in the rope."

I had a little puppy.
His name was Tiny Tim.
I put him in the BATHTUB,
to see if he could swim.

He drank all the water,
he swallowed
    a bar of soap.
Next thing you know,
it was halfway down his
THROAT.

In JUMPS the doctor.
In jumps the nurse.
IN JUMPS the lady with
the alligator PURSE.

Out jumps THE DOCTOR.
Out jumps the nurse.
OUT JUMPS the lady with
    the alligator PURSE.

TURNING JAPANESE

FOR FIVE YEARS in a row, Japanese teams have come in first place in the annual double-Dutch Holiday Classic in Harlem. No small feat, given the fact that before 1994, Japanese kids had never even heard of double Dutch. That year, an American team, the Unique Stylists, traveled to Japan as ambassadors of double Dutch. About twelve months later, the team they mentored, the Japanese Run D Crew went home with the top trophy. Japanese teams have been dominating the competition ever since.

Although the Tokyo teams tend to fare poorly in the speed competition, they shine in the Best of Show freestyle event, winning the judges' hearts with their gravity-defying flips, perfect splits, and Cirque du Soleil rope twirls. Unlike the American teams, which are made up primarily of teenage girls, the Japanese teams are evenly split between men and women and mostly feature participants in their twenties.

In Japan, double-Dutch jumpers tend to be lovers

> I wish I had a nickel.
> I wish I had a DIME.
> I wish I had a sweetheart
> who loved me all
> the time.
> I'd make him do the dishes.
> I'd make him sweep the floor.
> And when he got
> ALL finished,
> I'd KICK him
> OUT THE DOOR!

of hip-hop culture, choreographing their routines to an encyclopedic array of hip-hop beats, and sporting cornrows and baggy hip-hop gear in competition. There isn't a tournament circuit in Japan, but because double Dutch is so new in that country, the teams can earn a good living by performing on television and in front of live audiences. I spoke to leaders of two of Japan's world champion teams about their love of double Dutch and how they are so boldly turning the sport Japanese.

MIHO, LEADER OF J-TRAP

"I'VE LOVED DANCING since I was a little kid and studied it in college. A few years ago, I found a video of a double Dutch team from the U.S. No one had seen double Dutch in Japan and I thought it was amazing—like a new kind of dance. My friend and I taught ourselves how to jump by playing the video over and over again. We must have hit the PAUSE button a hundred times.

The great thing about double Dutch is that there are no rules. I love the dance element of the sport. When we jam in the freestyle competition, we do anything we want. It's so much fun!

BANANA, banana, **Banana** split. **WHAT** did you get in arithmetic? 10, 20, 30, 40, 50, 60, 70, 80 90, 100!

Banana, Banana, **BANANAS** for free. What **did** *you* get in **geometry**? 10, 20, 30, 40, 50, 60, 70, 80 90, 100!

"In Japan, double Dutch is such a new thing. People are excited because they've never seen it before. Japanese audiences keep challenging us to be better.

Going to Harlem for the Holiday Classic competition was like a movie. I videotaped everything—the people, the streets, the stores. We were so impressed with the black girls. They are so fashionable. We love their clothes and their braids.

In Japan, double Dutch is a sport for twenty-somethings. In Harlem, it's played by kids. Their muscles are so pliable and their rhythm is so fast. We can never beat them in speed because the young kids' bodies are built for double Dutch. We win in freestyle because we can do complex routines.

In Japan, double Dutch is for entertainment, not competition. We're a professional double-Dutch group here in Tokyo.

We called our team J-Trap, because we practiced every day under Jingu Bridge. The bridge is in the Harajuku section of Tokyo, where a lot of young people hang out. We took *J* for the bridge, and *Trap* is a play on the Japanese word for rope. We call ourselves J-Trap because we want to make a trap for our tricks with the rope.

Teddy Bear, Teddy Bear,
turn around.
TEDDY BEAR, Teddy Bear,
touch the ground.
Teddy Bear, Teddy Bear,
show your **shoe.**
Teddy Bear, Teddy Bear,
that will do.
TEDDY BEAR, Teddy Bear,
GO UPSTAIRS.
Teddy Bear, Teddy Bear,
say your prayers.
Teddy Bear, Teddy Bear,
turn out the light.
TEDDY BEAR, Teddy Bear,
say good night.

4 5

"We do our routines to old-school hip-hop and breakbeats. We also like to jump to Fatboy Slim. We mix so many different beats.

We would love to wear braids or dreads. But in Japan, it's so expensive, it can cost well over five hundred dollars to get your hair styled in dreads or braids. I usually wear my hair in a ponytail.

Japanese teams are almost more acrobatic. When we turn the rope, it's like something from a circus. If we have three minutes of performance, we vary the routine from very slow to very fast. We're always thinking about how the rope looks. We're trying to form a picture with the rope. It's art—not just in the way we jump, but in the way the ropes fly through the air."

> Down, DOWN, baby,
> down by the waterfront.
> Sweet, sweet baby,
> I'll never let you go.
> Shimmy, shimmy, cocoa
> POP.
> Shimmy shimmy, boom.
> Shimmy, shimmy, cocoa
> POP.
> Shimmy, shimmy,
> BOOM.

JUN, LEADER OF ABSOLUTE WISH

"WE USED TO PLAY jump rope pretty often when we were kids. At school, we used to play a lot, especially during the wintertime because we got warm easily from jumping. Lately, at Japanese elementary schools, more and more children have started playing double Dutch in physical-fitness classes, but teachers are not even aware that it's actually double Dutch.

"What I like about double Dutch is that it is a very new sport in Japan, with more style. I especially love it when an audience enjoys watching our performance. Also, there are few or maybe no sports that men and women can enjoy together.

Our team has five members now—three males and two females. All are twenty-two years old and seniors at Nippon Taiiku University. We chose the team name Absolute Wish, hoping that we could be number one in the world. We practice three times a week in a rented gymnasium at an elementary or junior high school because double Dutch has not yet been acknowledged as an official club at our university. We have very strict conditions to become an official club, such as, there must be more than thirty members, one advisor, contributions to university, etc. I think we can enter as an official club next year.

We use hip-hop music, but not just new songs. We also like music that is a little bit older. A lot of it is from the Sugar Hill record label. Most American players use recent hip-hop music, but we use music from the late eighties, so we can adopt break-dance style in double Dutch. Break-dance music is pretty up-tempo, and

Had a **little** bumper car, Number **48**. Went **around** the **corner**... and **SLAMMED** on **THE BRAKES.** **Policeman** came and put me in **jail.** **HOW** many days till I made bail?

Apples, peaches, **pears,** and **PLUMS,** tell me **when your BiRTHDAY** comes. **January,** February, March, **April, May,** JUNE, July, **August,** September, **October,** November, December.

47

we love to speed up performances along with the music. At our first award-winning Apollo Theater competition, though, we used the sound track of a Bruce Lee movie.

I have been wearing dreads and braids since I was a freshman in college. Last year, I got my hair braided in Harlem for the first time. We can't speak English well, so we just pointed out the style we wanted in their catalog. People at the salon seemed surprised to see five young Japanese coming in. That was fun. I couldn't believe that it took only two hours to get it done and was so inexpensive!

When I visited Harlem for the first time, I was just a kid, you know, a freshman at that time. We got off the subway on 125th Street and walked around, and many people on streets started conversations with us. We could not understand English and got a little bit scared. However, we got used to Harlem. We could tell the people were friendly.

The competition was held at the Apollo Theater in Harlem. It's a historic place to perform. I knew Lauryn Hill and Michael Jackson had sung there at amateur night. The audience was a lot different from ones we were used to at home. Japanese audiences are usually quiet, watching and focusing on performances, but the audience at the Apollo Theater expressed their feelings. They danced and shouted, which was really exciting and stimulating to us. We really enjoyed performing in that kind of atmosphere."

Ice-cream soda,
CHERRY on top.
Who's your boyfriend?
I forgot.

Tell me does it start
with an **A, B, C, D ...**

Not last night,
but the NIGHT before,
twenty-four robbers came
KNOCKING at my door.
I asked them what
they **wanted**
and this is what **they said:**
Spanish **DANCER,** do the
splits, splits, **splits!**
Spanish Dancer, do the
twist, TWiST, twist!
Spanish Dancer,
turn **AROUND,**
touch the **GROUND,**
and out the **back door.**

DOUBLE-DUTCH FRIENDSHIP

JENNY BEVILL, ART TEACHER, AND LILY GILES

JENNY: Growing up in Huntsville, Alabama, double Dutch was a huge part of my childhood. Now that my daughter, Lily, is learning to jump, I really understand the importance of double Dutch and how it can affect a girl's life. One of my first memories of elementary school was watching with admiration as my classmates double-Dutched during recess. The slapping sound of the rope hitting the ground, the rhythm and rhymes of their voices in unison, the laughter, the joy on their faces—I'll never forget it. I knew from that moment that I had to be a part of this special bond, the sisterhood nurtured between two twirling ropes.

When I look at it now, double Dutch was one of the few games that girls played where we learned some of the invaluable lessons of life: teamwork, coordination, cooperation, and confidence in our abilities. Even though jumping is the best part, you had to take your turn at the handles, which was very important. It's give-and-take, a back-and-forth rhythm much like dancing.

51

Lily is fortunate growing up used to seeing women who are physically active and involved in various sports. For me, there weren't many physical activities that girls could participate in and shine. There were no Little League, soccer, or basketball teams for girls, let alone any professional teams such as the WNBA.

Even though Lily participates in baseball and basketball teams outside of school, jumping rope is a big part of her day. When the bell rings for recess, she and her friends run past the Hula-Hoops, balls, and bats to the jump ropes. They don't know any of the traditional rhymes yet, and I'm sure they will make up some of their own. It was a very special day when Lily came home and shared that she had jumped through the alphabet, A to Z. The satisfaction in her voice and the confidence in her stance were priceless.

When Lily and I recently attended a good friend's double-Dutch—themed birthday party, Lily was totally embarrassed that I was out there jumping. She thought I looked so silly. I was just thrilled that I was able to jump as though I had never missed a day of doing it.

Miss Susie had a steamboat.
The steamboat had a bell.
MISS SUSIE went to Heaven.
The steamboat went to
Hello Operator,
PLEASE give me
number nine,
and if you disconnect me,
I'll paddle your
Behind the REFRIGERATOR,
There was a piece of glass,
Miss Susie sat upon it and
BROKE her little
Ask me no more questions.
Tell me no more lies.
The boys are in the bathroom
Pulling down their
Flies are in the meadow
BEES are in the PARK,
Miss Susie and her boyfriend
are kissing in the
D-A-R-K, D-A-R-K,
D-A-R-K,
DARK-DARK-DARK!

DESIREE: Growing up in the Bedford Stuyvesant section of Brooklyn, Rodney and I had a wonderful childhood. I don't remember when Rodney started jumping double Dutch, but when he did, we were all amazed. It was like, "Dang, Rodney is good." There were not a lot of games where you had to pick people to play, but when we wanted to double-Dutch, Rodney was the one we asked first. The joke about me was that it took me so long to get in the rope. I could turn, though, and that was fine with me! I would let Rodney jump in my place because I didn't want everyone to have to wait for me to jump in. I was a little shy about that, so I would just turn and chew my gum. With double Dutch, it's essential to chew gum and move your foot. It helps you keep your rhythm.

RODNEY: It wasn't that I didn't like to play other games, but my mom only let me play behind our building. The boys played basketball and baseball outside the area where I was allowed. I was athletic, though. I would jump to forty up and my stomach would be hurting, my heart would be burning, and I'd still be jumping. I

DEBBIE EGAN-CHIN

5 3

just had it in me to be the winner. My friendship with Desiree is like that—jumping longer than anyone could imagine.

ERIKA CLARKE, MTV PRODUCER
AND ADRIENNE HURST, PSYCHOLOGY INTERN

ERIKA: We met during orientation at NYU. We were both black girls from the suburbs who went to predominantly white schools. We've always gotten along very well without having to say much to each other. We understand each other's idiosyncrasies and craziness like no one else can. This was the first close friendship since elementary school that I'd had with another black female. Adrienne is the closest thing to a sister that I have.

ADRIENNE: We both know how to turn double Dutch, but we can't jump. Erika learned at some multiculti school she went to, and I learned when I visited my cousins in Philly. We're not exactly sporty, but we did learn. I used to feel bad that I couldn't jump double Dutch, but then I met Erika and it was like we made a team. You need two people to turn a rope.

54

DOUBLE LONGING

TEN YEARS BEFORE AIR JORDANS, I learned to fly. It's like the way brothers pimp-walk to a basketball hoop with a pumped-up ball and throw a few shots, hitting each one effortlessly. Like a car idling before a drag race, there is an invitation, perhaps even a threat, in the way their sneakers soft-shoe the pavement and the ball rolls around in their hands.

As double-Dutch girls, we had our own prance. Three of us and a couple of ropes. We knew the corners where you could start a good game. Like guys going up for a layup, we started turning nice and slow. Before jumping in, we would rock back and forth, rocking our knees in order to propel ourselves forward. It wasn't a question of whether we'd make it in, we'd conquered that years before. The challenge was to prove how long we could jump. The tricks we would do—pop-ups, mambo, around the world—were just for show, just to work the other girls' nerves. The real feat was longevity. So when we picked the corner where we were going to double-Dutch, we came with ropes and patience.

There is a space between the concrete and heaven where the air is sweeter

and your heart beats faster. You drop down and then you jump up again and you do it over and over until the rope catches your foot or your mother calls you home. You keep your arms to your sides, out of the way, so they don't get tangled in the rope. Your legs feel powerful and heavy as they beat the ground. When you mambo back and forth, it's like dancing. When you do around the world, it's like a ballet dancer's pirouette. In the rope, if you're good enough, you can do anything and be anything you want.

BEVERLY ROAD, GO SWINGING.
BEVERLY ROAD, GO SWING-ING.
BEVERLY ROAD, GO SWINGING,
BEVERLY ROAD, GO SWING-ING.

On my side of the street is where we jumped because Drena, who lived by me, had the best rope, and like cattle, we followed the rope. The best kind for

My name is (Girl's name).
I'm rough and tough.
If you mess with me,
I'll kick your butt.

Ooo, she thinks she's
bad.
Baby, I know I'm bad.
Ooo, she thinks
she's cool.
Cool enough to steal
your dude.

My name is (Girl's name).
I'm sassy and strong.
You turn the rope.
I'll jump all day long.

Ooo, she thinks she's fierce.
Baby, I know I'm fierce.
Ooo, she thinks she's good.
Good enough
to rule this 'hood.

jumping was telephone wire because it was light yet sturdy, and it hit the sidewalk with a steady rhythm. The telephone wire that connected your phone to the jack was not long enough. The only way to get telephone rope was from someone who worked for the telephone company. Drena's uncle was a telephone repairman, so she always had rope.

The worst kind of rope was the kind you bought in the store—cloth ropes with red plastic handles that came in plastic packages with pictures of little blond girls on them. First of all, they were too short. It would take two or three to make one side of a good double-Dutch rope. Second, the ropes were too soft for serious jumping (which only made sense because everybody knew that white girls were no kind of competition when it came to jumping rope). But in a clutch, you could run a soft rope under a hose and get it good and wet to make it heavier. The only problem was keeping it wet.

MISS MARY MACK-MACK-MACK
ALL DRESSED IN BLACK-BLACK-BLACK
WITH SILVER BUTTONS-BUTTONS-BUTTONS
ALL DOWN HER BACK-BACK-BACK.

We would split into teams. Only two positions: jumper and turner. You had to be good at both. No captain, just Shannon with her big mouth, and Lisa, who really couldn't jump, but talked a lot of junk. With two people turning and one person jumping and everybody else sitting around waiting for their turn, it wasn't hard to start a fight.

"Pick your feet up! Pick your feet up!"
"I hear you."
"Well then, act like it."
"You just mind your business, okay?"

Sometimes when I was jumping, I would catch someone on my team yanking the rope so she could call a time-out. Usually, it was Drena, because it was her rope and she thought that meant she didn't have to play fair. "Uh-huh. Start over. Jeanine is turning double-handed," Drena would say. To us, double-handed was something like being crippled or blind. When a double-handed person turned, the ropes would hit against each other, spiraling in lopsided arcs. It not only messed up our jumping, it looked ugly, shaky, and uneven. A good double-Dutch rope looked like a wire eggbeater in motion.

Five little **MONKEYS**
JUMPING on the **bed.**
One **fell off**
and **BUMPED**
his head.
Mama called
the doctor,
and the doctor said,
"*No more monkeys*
JUMPING on the **bed!**"

"It's okay. It's fine," I would say.

Drena wouldn't be swayed. "Veronica, don't try to cover up. Everybody on the block knows Jeanine is double-handed."

"Am not," Jeanine would mumble.

If there wasn't someone to take Jeanine's place, Drena would wrap up the rope and declare the game over. Then we'd go back to her house and watch TV. Drena was the only girl on the block to have her own room, plus a canopy bed, a dressing table, a TV, and a stereo. Staring blankly at *Gilligan's Island*, I would ask Drena, "Why'd you mess up the game? You know Jeanine is not double-handed." She would roll her eyes, "I'm so sick of those girls. I was just trying to get us out of there." But other times she would stick to her story and refuse to budge. "You know that girl is double-handed. Shut up and pass the Munchos."

Oooh, she thinks she's bad.
Baby, I know I'm bad.
Oooh, she thinks she's cool.
Cool enough to steal your dude.

We'd meet around 3:30, after we'd changed from our school clothes into our play clothes. Then we'd jump until the parents started coming home. Most of our parents worked nine to five in Manhattan and it took them an hour to get home. We knew it was coming up on six o'clock when we saw the first grown-up in business clothes walking down the hill from the Utica Avenue bus stop.

Sometimes a grown-up woman dressed in the stockings and sneakers that all our mothers wore for the long commute home would jump into the ropes—handbag and all—to show us what she could do. She usually didn't jump for very long; these women had no intention of sweating their straightened hair into kinkiness. But we always gave them props for still being able to get down. Secretly, I loved the way they clutched their chests, as if bras were useless in double Dutch, and the way their bosoms rose and fell in the up-and-down rhythm of the rope. I longed for the day when I would jump double Dutch and have something round and soft to hang on to.

Around this time, I would start looking out for my mother. I could usually spot her from two blocks away. In the spring, she wore her tan raincoat. In the fall, she wore the same raincoat with the liner buttoned underneath. I knew the purses she carried and the way she walked. If I hadn't made up my bed or if I was jumping in my good school clothes, I could usually dash into the house before she got there and do what I was supposed to do. If I wasn't in trouble, I'd try to make my turn last long enough so that my mother could see me jump.

"Wait, Mom, watch me jump!" I would say. Even though I knew she'd always say no.

"I've got to start dinner," she'd say. "And I've seen you jump before."

"But I've learned a new trick!" I'd say, trying not to sound like a baby in front of my friends.

But she wouldn't even turn around. She'd be carrying a plastic shopping bag that held her work shoes and the *Daily News*.

"Some other time," she'd say, closing the gate behind her.

There's so much I can do. So much stuff she doesn't know. But it's always some other time with her. Here is what I wish she knew: there is a space between two ropes where nothing is better than being a black girl. The helix encircles you and protects you, and there you are strong. I wish she'd let me show her. I could teach her how it feels.